Ellen Jaffe

Earth Day in Leith Churchyard
Poems in Search of Tom Thomson

For Ellen
love,
Bernadette

A Meditation on the Last Voyage of Herb Pohl

"Light is constant, we just turn over in it."
                                        Marilynne Robinson

A cloud-shrouded light
flows sideways
over the surfaces where we rest
here at the close of day

Our canoe is turning, as ever,
drawing us through glories of air
& mysteries of water

releasing us, over & over again
into what we hold sacred

Earth Day in Leith Churchyard

Poems in Search of Tom Thomson

by Bernadette Rule

Seraphim
EDITIONS

The publisher gratefully acknowledges the financial assistance of the Canada Council for the Arts and the Ontario Arts Council.

 Canada Council for the Arts **Conseil des Arts du Canada**   **ONTARIO ARTS COUNCIL CONSEIL DES ARTS DE L'ONTARIO** an Ontario government agency un organisme du gouvernement de l'Ontario

Library and Archives Canada Cataloguing in Publication
Rule, Bernadette, 1951-, author
    Earth Day in Leith Churchyard : poems in search of Tom Thomson / by Bernadette Rule.
ISBN 978-1-927079-38-6 (paperback)
    1. Thomson, Tom, 1877-1917–Poetry. I. Title.
PS8585.U54E37 2015   C811'.54   C2015-905479-6

Editor: Robert Priest
Front cover: *Byng Inlet, Georgian Bay* 1914 – 15 by Tom Thomson
              Image courtesy of the McMichael Canadian Art Collection
Back cover photo: Jim and Sue Waddington
Design and Typography: Julie McNeill, McNeill Design Arts

Published in 2015 by
Seraphim Editions
4456 Park Street
Niagara Falls, ON
Canada L2E 2P6

Printed and bound in Canada

Contents

Foreword

I have been fascinated by the work of Tom Thomson since 1977 when *Tom Thomson: The Silence and the Storm* by Harold Town and David P. Silcox was published. That book was my introduction to him. There was an immediacy to the paintings which I found totally captivating, and very different from the art to which I had been exposed before. I saw it as a kind of crash course in Canadian culture, having moved here from the States a year and a half earlier.

Then five years ago my daughter moved, first to Owen Sound, and then to Leith. Visits to her there afforded me the opportunity to explore Tom Thomson's life and work in more depth, beginning with an afternoon I spent in Leith Churchyard. I only realized later that I was there on Earth Day. That brought on the first poem, and the others followed in a steady flow as I studied his work, read about his life and visited the places that shaped and inspired him.

Thomson is a towering icon of Canadian art. His early and mysterious death is part of this, but more important is the work, which developed so rapidly over a five year period.

His favourite writer, Izaak Walton, said "As no man is born an artist, so no man is born an angler." Indeed, Thomson continued to learn, as a painter and as a naturalist, to the end of his life, and his learning in the last years was prodigious.

John Keats wrote almost every poem we know him for in a six-month period. But he knew he was dying, and that – plus falling in love with Fanny Brawne – seems to have fueled his remarkable achievement. The arc of Thomson's meteoric accomplishment is slightly different. His death was sudden and violent, and the counterpart to Fanny Brawne for him was Alice Elinor Lambert, whom he'd loved and lost some fifteen years before his death. There is no doubt that he was involved with Winifred Trainor at the time of his death, and possibly on the verge of marrying her, but that, too, is left out of focus and has become part of the mysterious legend of Tom Thomson's final year. What is clear is the power of the work, and his love of the Ontario landscape, particularly Algonquin Park. Exploring this through poetry has been a joy.

Bernadette Rule

"Moonlight Over Canoe Lake"
Tom Thomson Paints his Murderer

He fingerprints the clouds
that try to thumb the moon aside
in favour of darkness,

clouds that flow so quickly overhead
they could easily cause him
to lose balance. But he stands tall

The hills on the distant shore
lie like slain bodies,
unmoving & unmoved

He does not turn away
but watches the drama unfold
daubing footprints of moonlight

across Canoe Lake,
clues that lead directly
to a dull & bloodless hole in the night

Mapping Abstraction

This double-page spread of pastels
is an abstract portrait of fictional shapes –
territory & province – sky-tinted networks of water
breaking it up, holding it together
oceans, rivers, lakes, the great
blue hooray of Hudson's Bay

More aquagraphy than geography

What is a border when you cross it?
A fluid idea whose strongest image
is in these big blocks of colour
on the prettiest page of the atlas

The Iris Opening

A loon call flutes the morning
hollows out the fog & pipes the light

It's the very sound
of the eyes' dilation

It's what I long to paint

May, 1912

The trees are busy
with buds that hive the light
in cells of golden green

Each day my palette
blossoms with more colour

Skipping Breakfast

The air this morning's a clear glass of whiskey
It diverts & enriches me
as the tree branch fattens the rain drop

I push deeper into the woods
drunk on beauty

Joyous Homecoming

The geese beat across
a wilderness of sky

As the taut string breaks
they drop with off-key cries of triumph
to a lake whose name they know

They sit up late like we do
talking & talking

Leaf Sky Shine

The canoe is a leaf on a silken sleeve
all glisson & sweetly weightless
sky & water silver on silver
small gulps at the prow
dripshine off a paddle

In silent thrall
I've slipped sideways
between two kinds of light

Colour Sleeping

These stones hold
in their grey embrace
all the colours of the world
Beneath the lake they're purple
orange pink green blue
Drying on the shore
they dream the spectrum still
behind closed eyes

Burnt

This one
dead tree,
lightninged
black
lends drama
to the well-dressed rest

"Red Rocks, Georgian Bay"

Great stones fill the slope
leading to the lake
They glow like a still life of Easters

How long have they held this balance
rolling in slow motion toward eternity's shore

"Evening, Canoe Lake"

While dusk stains the birches lavender
I paint my tent
as no more
than one crouching
stone among the many others
beside the lake

which is disappearing
into its music

stilling for sleep

"Blustery Morning"

Written in the wind's italic script
on an undulating page
these cedars reaching outward
over the escarpment edge
honour the flowing river
ancestrally it seems,
trunks & bark both twisting
as they turn & bow in dreams

"Summer Clouds"

For art, the morning's built a range of cloud
to match the mountains time has made of stone
as thoughts are echoed when we speak aloud
or flesh restates the hidden lines of bone

& shadow's playful replica of form
reminds us what we see may not be real –
at least not all there is to life's brief storm
Laminations strengthen & conceal

But Nature's way of echoing each shape
can draw us ever onward in some task
from which we never, in the end, escape,
the horizon moving just beyond our grasp

We need not choose which mountain range to climb
Both stand & melt on either side of time

Preparation

A blue storm is balanced
on the fir tips

A rabbit runs into the bush
But the birds are silent

carrying the weight of the wait

Storm in Four Movements
with Appended Scherzo

A leaf turns down the wind
The deciduous chorus sighs

Kettledrum & harpstring,
the storm opens over the lake

The more muted passage
folds the wings of firs,
its white noise
identical to silence

At last the crescendo
separates into notes
which scamper up the scale
                     as they taper off

Inexplicable,

the power of sudden sunlight
on a birch trunk already tagged
                              by its own unravelling

Lonesome

From my camp I hear the train
blowing its trinity note of loss
into the harmonica of the midnight horizon

Deep vibrations follow for a time
wheels on rails. It sets the wolves howling
Reminds me of fundamentals:

my mother's heartbeat
heard from within her body,
her blood rushing all around me as I formed

Meals

Scattered across the big rock
a gull's breakfast
carapace of crab
its orange shell becoming blue
articulated limbs toylike, clever

Brilliance wasted, or maybe just finished

In the end it's all about that grasp
those opposable claws, the jointwork:
inventions in support of supper

Back Home

From the doorway of the church
I survey the fields of my childhood,
now farmed by others

They've worked all week
to open the earth for seed
It's fat as a goose-down mattress
fragrant as a barn full of cattle

& we stand & watch it steam
in the evening's change of season

By God, I love this land
Tame or wild, I love
this pregnant land

Seasons

I would archive light's ovulation,
ending at the beginning

from summer's green flags
to the maples' autumn celebration

through the banked fires of winter
to the cherry's bridal fall toward the stream

"Early Spring"

In these woods white trees stand
against sloping ground still white with snow
under a mostly white sky

All we have
for colour on this white page
is the blue ink of shadows

It's enough

Handiwork

A glove lies beside the trail
its entrails pilfered for nests

In every fork & hollow
spring building advances

The woodpecker's *tok-tok-tok*
bounces across the water

to where a nest, like one of Aunt Betty's hats,
is being made over

One could almost believe the birds
are stealing wisps of cloud for nesting

as more & more blue
shows through

Study

This is the time when the fruit trees
part their green lips
with a glimpse of pink tongue

like children leaning over homework
forcing their new brilliance
onto the lined pages assigned them

Summer, 1914

We've portaged the pine
to those caught
in the sharp-edged trap of the city:

spacious skies
Canadian Shield
scalloped shores of Algonquin
this mansion featuring broad stone stairs
                            with runners of bright water

We built windows onto wild open spaces
& carried them out over alvar & muskeg
for those who cannot get here themselves

"Northern River"

Through a screen of scraggly spruce
one fallen & all dark
we glimpse light's chalice,
a promise of redemption
improbable, wild & gleaming

"Burned Over Land"

Four black totems rise
from ground that cradles yet
the fire that consumed it

Shield stones pulsing like embers
in the banked sunset

"In Algonquin Park"

Each leaf on the foreground branch
is the size of the clouds
pendant over the open water
& equally important
in this invoice
of waves, landforms, clouds,
branches all reaching, flowing,
weaving the wild

A restless brightness resides
in the broad-stroked light,
captured on a piece of wood
which might've been used to raise
another kind of radiance

"The Rapids"

A white outcry pitches
against the dark still
background of forest

Great rocks sleek as whales
seem to shape the spume & suds
that fly around them

The surprise is
it's the other way around

"The Waterfall"

Encountered through deep woods
this canted column of silver sound
stands mysterious as an apparition

the spirit of the land itself
as it pours in place
among these rocks & trees

Owen Sound through a Kitchen Window

Through winter trees
a small town twinkles in its vale
like an unzipped change purse
tipped this way & that in the shop

Buildings form a pattern
of red & ochre blocks,
each a smear of paint
lending colour to the townscape

Trees & distance abstract the scene
to its proper value, to what it is:

its own sort of alvar,
a colony of rich growth
on the rock-paved shore
of something great

Proportion

Piecemeal upon the fallen leaves
as if across a shattered pane
the last of the day's appointed light
falls on the path behind

Slowly the forest absorbs a day
accepting & creating change,
exchanging gold for silver
at the threshold of two worlds

Then all that thrive in halls of night
open wings & petals wide
to welcome their separate, dark release
into the hours of time they lease

'til moon & stars decant again
the last of their apportioned light
through the latticework of trees
piecemeal upon the fallen leaves

Hunger

In the morning I'll waken
to flapjacks and eggs at Mowat Lodge
then strike out for the deserted
lumber camp near the river's mouth

They'll have carved out a space
where I can sit all day
studying a new & lateral view of the woods

I vow I'll have twisted
every tube of paint in my box
before the Frasers' fish fry tomorrow night

Migrations at Mowat Lodge

Shannon & Annie & I sit up late by the fireplace
absorbing the firewater in our glasses

Upstairs the others turn in their own dreams
releasing from the bedsprings chevrons of honking geese

which fit the roofline for just an instant
before rising to intersect with stars

Getting There

The deer path barely parts these tall grasses
I can smell their bodies, see their beds
& know they slept here just last night

How to paint that smell, the call of birds,
the warmth of sun across my hand
as I lift a fresh-dipped brush to an empty board

Shattered

I've been weeks among rapids and jack pine
trying to memorize each hour's
slanted light among the branches,
every turn of wind over the water

I lay paint onto these little birch boards
thick as fish scales – hell, thick as their fins
but it can't come up to the dream
I'm standing in

Suddenly, knowing it's all no good,
I pick up my paintbox
and hurl it as far as I can into the trees

All night long I imagine
bears or their racoon cousins
eating my paints, birds plucking
at my brushes for their nests

every sound in the bush
erasing sleep until finally, finally

I drop off, only to dream empty pictures,
galleries and galleries of empty frames

At dawn, stiff with cold,
I follow the arc of that anger
'til, dew-drenched, I see my tools
scattered at the base of a spruce

& run, gathering up every last tube and brush
to hold against my stupid, pounding heart

"Byng Inlet, Georgian Bay"

In the old tale when the wind
& the sun compete, the sun wins
Out here the wind wins

In its constancy it sat for me
I've made a portrait of this spirit
this great transparent holy ghost

whose stroke has formed
these very stones & every tree & bush,
taught junipers their sideways reach

For the portrait it donned the season's changes
sharp spring green
against the cedars' patient dark

The big pines, built like harps
play their master's music
as with its breath it shapes the sky itself

Canoeing the Rapids

This is as close as I can come to being
salmon, the river's silver soul

& as the white spray rises round me
I know what it is to be

the object of the fisherman's desire,
the subject of the artist's flying brush

Field Guides

Your Izaak Walton in your pocket
you fished, canoed & hiked
across Ontario
                    This was before
Roger Tory Peterson invented field guides,
pocket references to birds, trees, wildflowers

When you were collecting your data
Peterson was a child, roaming
his part of upstate New York
not far – as the crow flies –
from where you roamed

a child the authorities exempted
from the wartime curfew
(as the authorities exempted you from school)
because they knew this distractedly focused boy
who needed to sketch every bird & leaf
that came under his intense gaze
They knew they couldn't keep him
indoors

He was nine when you died
having left your own field guides
in oil. Having seen the forest
                    & the trees

Colour

The bush isn't colourless. Anything but.
In every season it's suffused
with an aching, prismatic
beauty all its own.

Even winter birches cast a spell
of pink light.
But to come upon these wildflowers
bursting from the dominant green ...

All I can do is kneel,
open my paintbox
& lean in close
to honour colour.

"The Jack Pine"

Don't talk to me of sophistication,
elegance, grace. I can show you
candelabra
          grand piano
                    curving staircase
in one great tree that grows beside the lake.

Critique

If I said he painted water
through a tracery of branches
you'd imagine something
delicate & light

If I said he laid on colour
like a heavy patchwork quilt
you might think he had no
subtlety or skill

It's painting without drawing
but it works
The man's half unschooled wilderness
& so's his bloody work. So tell me,
why the hell is it so good?

Landscapes

Where are the bears, people ask,
moose, deer, wolves?

They're here, I tell you
in rockface & trees,
hidden by leaves
like Adam & Eve.
They're in the very shape
of this landscape.

Can't you see?

"In the Northland"

This place is birches built around a lake
as a bird is feathers built around a song

The raspberry bursaries of evening
stain the whole bowl of the sky
Summer fattens on
deciduous clouds, cumulous trees

In the east, half a moon hangs
stained with its birth
whole in its brokenness

Chevron

Just
above me
the tent peaks,
a portaged canoe.

Always this shape recurs:
the summit of the balsam fir,
the vee of the geese flying over,
river & road & rails as they merge
at the horizon, colour's final upward
surge, as the aurora borealis tapers off.
Tent peg, arrowhead, beaver-chewed
stump. Whether inlet or peninsula,
it's this shape we must return to,
the peaked roofline of home,
the place where we began:
delta of female passion,
beloved place of birth.
Breast. Mountain.
Campfire flame.
Shim. Wedge.

Niche.
Urge.

Crepuscular Catch

Near dawn I climb out of the tent to pee
A bird, torn from the night,
flaps raggedly toward morning

Beyond it a shooting star
highlights the stillness of the rest
nested in their invisible orbits

Deeply I inhale woodsmoke
& turpentine, last year's crushed pine needles,
the cool breath of the lake itself

As schools of light rise to sip
the morning air, I get to work
casting nets of paint over boards of birch

News, 1915

Jackson's gone to the war,
the war that wouldn't take me

Last year on the train north we studied the map
strategizing where to make camp
how to capture wind & weather with a brush

Imagine, paid to paint for a year!
We were traveling to the wilderness,
off to harvest a crop of light, filled with ferocious joy

Now he's on his way to another wilderness, sure to harvest
some darkness, offering his life on the altar of this country
I dread to think that we might one day get the grim word
of his death. It's enough to bring you back
to your parents' prayers

"Round Lake, Mud Bay"

Against a citrus sky
I watch a lone goose labour
to join the group ahead
flapping his great weight
up invisible slopes,
the others calling, *Come on!*

Finally he joins them
making their checkmark a vee
& I feel with sudden pain
the absence of my friends

Harness

Morning light lies
in fixed grids across this shack
in the middle of Toronto
where I've set out the last of my
bread & coffee for breakfast

The city outside is gearing up
for something wider than its parsed sky,
its brilliant purpose a mystery to me
as I try to remember
Huron's tortured shoreline
onto the stretched canvas
It's like wrestling a white pine
inside a tent

The milkman's horse clops past
I look around to see him
trussed up in his harness,
pulling his load. Turning
back to the empty canvas
I knock the coffee over
smashing the cup into four pieces

A dark, fragrant rivulet
seeks the lowest place

Stomach growling,
I mix up a storm
on the palette

"The Birch Grove, Autumn"

Algonquin has its parthenons
rising from the massive
Precambrian Shield,
tesserae of turquoise overhead

The Shield itself a cracked acropolis,
creation's forge fires cradled
in foundation stones for stately halls
like this one

This must be what the ancients
were trying to reconstruct –
columns of light slanting
through columns of white

A temple to Nature & Colour
iconic, timeless, holy,
bearing in block letters
the architect's bold stamp

"Northern Lights"

It begins with a quick of light
at the horizon, nail bed
of the thumb of Angel Gabriel
coming to blow us home

Wolves howl somewhere not far off
& I feel an answer rising in my throat,
some old call & response
the voyageurs would understand

Stars are out in thousands
watching, almost silenced
as this new diffused light
enters the darkness

Some unseen source
spills green fire down the sky
More flares lick like a gas ring
against blue-black heavens

I add explosive whispers to the uproar,

run into the cabin & tell Robinson,
sketch it in the dark to repaint in the morning
But in the morning I see that it's there

"The West Wind"

The wind's penmanship
is legible in these cursive trees,
copper plate script of waves,
chorus of scrawling cloud
prophesying some dark climax
Even the stones flow in place

I alone keep still
as I read this written world
moving, finally, only
to translate it into paint

"Nocturne"

The world in darkness is still
the world. Without the moon
it looks at first like absence
but I feel its presence pulsing

As listening begins in silence,
seeing begins in darkness
One hand reaching out,
I cross the invisible threshold

"Snow in October"

Damp snow crosshatches
over unshed leaves
like woven sunbeams,
like something edible –
hashed browned potatoes or a lattice crust pie

The light through the branches
opens windows in the snow
& makes an early winter
almost welcome

Year End Inventory

You've reckoned it perfectly:
the pin oaks' copper;
the rolled nickels and dimes of the coming storm;
the unspent gold of the tamaracks.

We're almost out of the red.
Soon the ledger will be
totally black on white.
Good work.

Snowstorm

So much light
falling from darkness

Returning to Algonquin in Early Spring

Tonight's stars shine
cold as an urban nocturne
over a world still at war

You and I linger at the fireside
working out a love song which warms
better than the flames, invites risk

No one else is here. My heart
stumbles with the notes, catches in my throat,
stirs shadows from another time

Sixty-two Days:
A Final Record of Spring

Blue cracks shatter winter's shell
Rocks are chocolate with meltwater
Smashed panes of ice fall through lakes

The final snow – entwined with its fraternal twin,
rain – is gone by noon
Now the trees look taller, the sky steps back

Standing water turns the world upside down
Birds come home

Holding on to the Cottage
at Hope Bay

Soft escarpment against plum clouds

Ice inside the water's folds

Birches & snow

A great rock in the throat of the lakeshore

Memory against this landscape

Perspective

The centre can be anywhere
Let's say it's here
& that all the lines
curve across this land
from oceans & glaciers
over mountains & cities
to meet in this one body of water,
the space this lake creates

the vanishing point

where a ghost-grey canoe
floats upside down still
though it has long since worn away
to a transparent framework of ribs
arching like two hands tented in thought

It was probably burned as firewood

No one knows
Still, let's say it's here

where water & sky seem to meet
where trees grow out of bare rock

where the unthinkable
                        took place

Recipe for Angels

Just past dawn
pour intensities of sunlight
onto the last of the snowbanks

& watch as they rise
their auras unfolding ever outward
lingering especially about the beds of rivers

filling the air with grace
for a short while
before disappearing again

into even
           thinner
                    air

Earth Day in Leith Churchyard

The world out here has all gone to birds
birds of every size & colour & call
the air all a-scissor with wings
They wade up the river or scallop lightly
over the shore of the lake

& in Leith Churchyard
robins tumble in the cedar boughs
A turkey paces the copse
The river, with its own blue heron
crooks around us

A flock of Canadas arrows overhead
There's even a small iron bird
perched in art's still perfection
at the base of Tom Thomson's tombstone
on the grave that cannot hold him

Acknowledgements

I owe many a debt of gratitude for support and encouragement in the writing of *Earth Day in Leith Churchyard*. I thank everyone who has helped me, and I want to thank the following by name:

- Maureen Whyte of Seraphim Editions for saying yes
- Trudi and George Down of The Book Band
- Julie McNeill and Robert Priest for their help in crafting the book
- Tobi Bruce, Laurie Kilgour Walsh and the Art Gallery of Hamilton staff for remarkable generosity and warmth
- David Huff and everyone at the Tom Thomson Art Gallery in Owen Sound
- Wendy Campbell at the McMichael Gallery in Kleinburg
- Trina Chatelain and the staff at the Algonquin Park Visitor Centre
- Roy McGregor for sharing his comprehensive knowledge of Tom Thomson
- Jim and Sue Waddington for their book *In the Footsteps of the Group of Seven*

- Paul Lisson, Fiona Kinsella and Noelle Allen for their generosity and encouragement
- The Ontario Arts Council
- Bob Yates for rich conversation, amazing artwork and for his song "Tom Thomson's Mandolin"
- The Yates family for providing me with a strong, early welcome to Canadian culture
- Adam, Alvaro, Barbara, Beth, Duane, Francis, Jean, John, Jeffery, Jo, Krista, Lise, Richard, Stan, and all my fellow writers and artists for advice and comradeship worthy of the Group of Seven
- Everyone at Bryan Prince Bookseller (past and present), for being there and always supporting writers
- Glenna Jansen, Carol Leigh Wehking, Brenda Stephenson and Johanna Kuyvenhoven for unforgettable visits to Beckanon Island
- Carys for moving to Owen Sound, and Carys and Martin for sharing with me the perfect place from which to explore Tom Thomson's life and work
- Justin, Ross, Carys, Eamonn, Bridget, Rosie, Angela, Tim, Ronnie and all my family for unfailing support and inspiration, passion for art, hours of listening and sharing, laughter and love